The Plagiarist

poems by

Amy Schrader

Finishing Line Press
Georgetown, Kentucky

The Plagiarist

Copyright © 2017 by Amy Schrader
ISBN 978-1-63534-165-2 First Edition
All rights reserved under International and Pan-American Copyright Conventions.
No part of this book may be reproduced in any manner whatsoever without written
permission from the publisher, except in the case of brief quotations embodied in critical
articles and reviews.

ACKNOWLEDGMENTS

The author gratefully acknowledges *Pontoon Poetry*, in which "Cat's Eye (I)" and
"The Symbols" first appeared.

Publisher: Leah Maines

Editor: Christen Kincaid

Cover Art: Jamie Wilson

Author Photo: Jamie Wilson

Cover Design: Elizabeth Maines McCleavy

Printed in the USA on acid-free paper.
Order online: www.finishinglinepress.com
            also available on amazon.com

Author inquiries and mail orders:
Finishing Line Press
P. O. Box 1626
Georgetown, Kentucky 40324
U. S. A.

Table of Contents

The Plagiarist...1

Revision 2

Re- Vision 3

The Story..4

How It Happened 5

A Warning 6

Palimpsest..7

An Invitation...8

Cat's Eye (I)...9

Cat's Eye (II) 10

The Robber Bride..11

Mercator Map..12

Prosthesis...13

Symbolic 14

The Symbols 15

The Actual Symbols..16

How It (Really) Happened...17

Isabella Stewart Gardner Museum 18

Self-Portrait with Lions...19

Circular Reasons...20

Eve Again 21

A Curse 22

A Blessing 23

All Hallows' Eve..24

Notes on the Text..25

I stole your manuscript
just because I could.

—Terry Ann Wright, "Thief"

The Plagiarist

In the end, your crimes weren't original.
If you wrote our history, it would be
cliché: The Friendship. The Love Triangle.
In Eden we ate the fruit from the Tree

of Knowledge. The oldest story. *Ho hum.*
And now you're stealing my best lines. I guess
the husband turned, sonnet-like, away from
both of us eventually. Even this

form of theft's a sort of love letter.
Our verses *versus*. Our hatred uncut.
I was there first. I was there better.
I did not believe you until now, but

you are Rhoda to my Mary, since I'm
the one with reasons. The one with rhymes.

Revision

I break another wine glass in the sink.
My palms are bleeding. I suppose you think

I'd call it *stigmata*. More like *stigma*.
We age and start to question all our dogma.

Two sides to a story, always, and then
the truth. Therefore: I break another wine

glass at the bar. I break another
wine glass, cut my lip. I recover

gracefully, and grateful no one sees.
The other drinkers witness bloody knees,

the chip in my front tooth. Everyone
judges. Everyone is judged. Attention

is reality, asleep or awake.
I break another wine glass. How I break.

Re- Vision

Reminded, regret.
Rehash. Roulette.

Repurpose, as in
reuse, revise. Re-spin

the wheel of fortune; you
forgot to reference who

really wrote the lines.
This doesn't redefine

what happened. A recall
notice isn't possible,

nor are rehab, remix,
do-over. Knee-jerk reflex

to a knife in the navel.
Revenge is living well.

The Story

The story of the pot and kettle.
And yes, a story set in locker bays.
Pistols at dawn, or we could arm-wrestle
over a no-count boy. The old clichés.

I have been high before. What would you know
about it? A toke or hit, a shot
of whiskey, artful images, tableaux
of angels and the devil. (You are not

the *angels*, by the way.) Let's be clear.
The story of two women, ex-best friends
who somehow got *perverse* from *persevere*.
Who can say if we regret? In the end,

it all comes down to no-win choices,
and each of us has picked her poison.

How It Happened

In the miniature laboratory
of panic, as winter struck us.
The Bunsen burner an allegory
for warmth. We held our hands close.

All night the hollow bell of ego
tolled. Rather, hung in the tower.
Broken chords, arpeggios
made us long for naves and altars.

Or maybe the voiceless dog of faith,
debarked and kept in the kennel.
A kind surgeon scalpeled and stitched
it up. An accident, the surgical

clamp left deep inside us. Don't pick at
the scab. You know what happens next.

A Warning

But what if it is always winter?
I will admit that you are always there
beneath the surface of my mind: splinter
just beyond the tweezer's reach; in the air

surrounding me. It's getting colder
every day. You are the misery
in my lower back, arthritic shoulder,
ten ice-numbed fingers, and my tricky knee.

It gives out from time to time. It's weak.
By which I mean, sometimes I fall.
I should never touch the window. It leaks
and sticks in place. The view from here is small,

like your heart. Like mine. The season turns
unkind. The brittle kindling burns and burns.

Palimpsest

An itch, a scratch across the surface
of my thin skin. For years, I've tried to wash
my hands of it, to lay down the burden
of interpretation. I mean *backlash*.

I mean *accusation* and a trail
of clues. Our stories were the same stories,
slightly askew. Call it heretical:
we have to burn the books. Leave no copies.

You are the *scriptio inferior*,
the underwriting. You undermined me.
I am the faint remains of the former
text. Trace of smoke. I'm ghost-like, absentee.

It's as if I have always carried you
inside and out: black mark, bloodstain, tattoo.

An Invitation

The light within me honors the light within you.

To dedicate my practice to someone
absent—someone I love (or have loved
in the past)—I must set my intention.
As if all her sins (and mine) can be absolved

by opening my heart. Surgery
without the scalpel, gristle, tendon, bone.
But she nicked a major artery
and I'm not skilled enough in stitches. So

I've bled for years and I'm still bleeding.
I always go along to get along.
(Downward-Facing Dog takes on new meaning.)
I can admit that I'm not good or strong

enough to forgive her or forget her.
Palms in. *Namaste, you motherfucker.*

Cat's Eye (I)

I was not sorry for her, however
and however you want to think about
forgiveness…well, it's not as if she ever
asked for it. For years I rationed out

my gall. A poison dropped-by-drop, a wasp
in black and yellow. Sleek, carnivorous,
and on the prowl. So I began to grasp
the fact that women can be ravenous.

Or is it ravishing? Perhaps it's both.
I drew a line in the sand. Yes, I dared
her to take a step and now I'm loathe
to admit that I'd kind of hoped she would.

I drew a circle in the sand. Knuckled down
and shot hard. Knocked her out and shot again.

Cat's Eye (II)

It's the story that we could have written
but it already was. We knuckled down
so long ago that I forgot: *once bitten,
twice shy.* You were always skipping town

or skipping stones across the water.
A lark, a sudden raven on the branch,
the gutted pigeon: all were augurs
of your poison and your kindnesses.

Sometimes a hit's a *kiss*, sometimes a *kill.*
I kept my heart, my secret and best self,
locked up in a red purse. It was safe until
stolen. I thought you knew what it was worth.

I wanted to be friends. I said: *No quitsies.*
I didn't know we were playing for keepsies.

The Robber Bride

It's the story that we could have written
but it already was. One way of reading
it lets you be some kind of guardian
angel and I'm not broken or bleeding

but saved from an unworthy man. So thanks
for that, I guess. He was a minor
character at any rate. This smacks
of twisted sisterhood, a designer

brand of feminism where the mean girl
doesn't really mean it. Or does. I'll be
the one who reads backwards and studies war.
You know which one you are. You're also me,

or trying hard. Revise the fairy tale:
the bad girl, the red dress, a wedding veil.

Mercator Map

To take something round and flatten it.
Projections will distort the truth
of surfaces or size and bit by bit
we move away from the center. Our youth

becomes infinite, frayed at the edges.
To take something primal from each other.
The taking a theft, a gift, the wreckage
of a ship surrounded by sea monsters.

We're lost, adrift. We try to navigate
our shared experience, the war stories
inside our minds. But we exaggerate;
and keep our incomplete inventories

of all the wounds and weapons. We're crazy
to hope we'll ever reach land safely.

Prosthesis

Fake, like a limb attached
by buckle and straps.

If you are the stump, I am
the socket. We're door and jamb.

A key to its lock.
And if lost then picked,

jimmied, or jury-rigged.
The jury's been gagged

and sequestered for years.
The jury's hung and here's

the crux of it, the heart,
a sad story's saddest part:

I've never become numb
to you, dear itch and phantom limb.

Symbolic

> *A word is elegy to what it signifies.*
> —Robert Hass, *"Meditation at Lagunitas"*

A throwing together; a casting
of dice; the stroke of a missile, a bolt
or beam. Comparing and contrasting.
There has always been a double aspect:

a Rhoda to each Mary, bloody palm
for every nun. We're so desperate
to know if the other is genuine,
find out if we're the same or disparate.

The outward signs can be misleading.
We return to the idea of self-
image over and over. Find meaning
in plastic owls, a box on a shelf,

green apple. A smile becomes a weapon.
Our story becomes the stuff of legends.

The Symbols

Insomniac's waking dream: black cat,
the fulcrum of a fight. Bad luck. Look at

all we've saved in cardboard boxes and moved
across the country: the diary which proved

the infidelities, the folded notes
passed in the hall, the braided (quote, unquote)

friendship bracelet. Well, we never really
had one, did we? Phallic calla lily—

funereal—or is that the sword
lily? Gladiolus. Showy, unfurled,

let loose like your dark curls. And more abstract:
the wine glass, the cabernet, sex act

at the back of the pool hall. You were late.
I was worried. It's kind of hard to explain.

The Actual Symbols

The plastic owl,
                    the howl
of raccoons in the tree.
                    They sound like babies
or cats crying. A spiral
                    notebook: your diary.
I stole it. I'd do it again.
                    The Parisian
way you tied my scarf, loose
                    and blowsy. Close
call. Call girl, calling
                    home and jingling
quarters in her purse.
                    The red purse.
No, a red jacket. You wore
                    it to the Vineyard, on the shore.
A windy day. The wind
                    unwound us. We're still
unwinding.

How It (Really) Happened

A billow of birds—let's call them pigeons,
or maybe not—flap a sudden turn up
or away or backwards. Decisions
are made and then the unmaking. The cup

knocked onto the kitchen floor. The shatter
and glue. The inevitable way
the pieces wouldn't fit. Doesn't matter,
or so we thought: the leak or slip or stray.

Meaning *hair* or *dog*. Or *of*. The winter
light faded, slid behind the horizon.
Or maybe it was dawn, the sun a splinter
of crimson in an otherwise dark span

of sky. We realized that we were wrong
and absolutely right. We played along.

Isabella Stewart Gardner Museum

The largest theft in world history.
In Boston. I mean the largest *art* theft.
Among others. An unsolved mystery.
The art heist, anyway. Self-portrait

or mirror? I've long since given up
the effort to understand the difference.
Between us. Between this coffee cup
and the ceramic breaking. The silence.

Vermeer's *The Concert* the most valuable
one stolen. The one you took? Not so much.
The mere thought of ransom was laughable
even then. But I've always liked the Dutch

Masters. Domestic scenes, the table after
the hunt: bloody rabbits, scattered feathers.

Self-Portrait with Lions

The females are the hunters. We know this
and yet we shadow. We reflect. We call
it pride before a fall. Lean in and kiss
the mirror, smearing red. A stain, the fall

from grace: the apple, apple, apple. Blame
ourselves for the rest of our lives. Such crack,
such shatter. The skewed way a maiden name
appears in a convex curve. No going back.

We covet, and covet long curly hair.
We covet claws. We covet all the things
that we already have. A love affair
with what exists outside the frame: torn wings,

tall grass, the weakest prey. Put an ear up
to the wall. They're giving chase and catching up.

Circular Reasons

When I drink too much, I tell the story
                         to anyone at the table.
When I drink too much,
                         I tell the story again
and again. When I drink
                         too much I tell. I tell you,
I drink too much and I blame you.
                         Can you tell?
I used to write about Eve and how she fell.
                         I meant to write *to write about you.*
Let's drink this evening, to Eve
                         and how she fell. I tell
myself next week, I certainly
                         won't drink. I think
I'm catching up, catching
                         up to myself. Therefore,
I'm telling you.

Eve Again

> *...the screech owl also shall rest there, and find for herself a*
> *place of rest.*   —*Isaiah 34:14*

Of course I used her as a symbol
for myself. I imagined her as good
with words, after naming animal
and animal and animal. I should

have done my research sooner. She was not
the mate, but merely rib. Cartilage
and bone, honed to sharpness. An afterthought.
Lilith was the wife, the same earth and age

as Adam. Also demon, night creature,
the dirty hag. There she shall rest and lay,
under a shadow. Hatches and gathers
and cries out to her fellow birds of prey.

I placed a plastic owl on the deck
to scare the dirty pigeons off. (Home wreck.)

A Curse

I wasn't talking about you, you dog.
I meant myself. I meant I cried a lot.
I meant I wanted things. I nagged and clawed.
I meant I knotted a Gordian knot

around the marriage bed. A home to wreck?
It all depends upon your point of view.
It was my tomb and my haunted object
exhumed from the dark earth but somehow you

opened your mouth with a skeleton key.
I guess it doesn't matter now which version
of the story makes it into print. We
were almost exactly the same person.

When we said the same thing at the same time:
Jinx, you owe me a Coke.

A Blessing

I still curse all the time; proverbial
mouth of a sailor. A different kind
of incantation, the paranormal
casting of a spell, or fishing line

to catch a measure or two of comfort.
Not forgiveness, exactly, or favor
from God. More like noticing the colors
of the falling leaves in October.

October's for dying. I'll put to rest
all of my bitterness. Perhaps not all,
but most and also most of my regret.
What you did to me got me here. Long haul

to southern places in the heart. The calm
and quiet; gratitude after the storm.

All Hallows' Eve

There's Eve, again. I cannot seem to get
away from her. You could say she haunts me.
That's true enough. I'll light a cigarette
and strike a sad pose on the balcony.

No, wait, that's Juliet. Different
story with a different end. We're not
so different, you and I. Deliberate
on your part and perhaps on mine. Blind spot

let me overlook all the times you lied.
Decades later, I still don't have an answer
to any of my questions (e.g. *Why?*)
In the end, it doesn't really matter

which one of us he loved, or loved the most,
or loved at all. You are my favorite ghost.

Notes on the Text

The first line of "Cat's Eye (I)" is taken from the Margaret Atwood novel of the same name.

Amy Schrader holds a B.A. in Molecular & Cell Biology and English Literature from the University of California at Berkeley, and an M.A. in English Literature from Boston University. She earned her M.F.A. in poetry from the University of Washington.

Her poems can be found in *Bone Bouquet, Rattle, Unsplendid, The Monarch Review, Bateau, DIAGRAM, The Journal, Willow Springs*, and elsewhere. Her chapbook *The Situation & What Crosses It* was published in 2014 by MoonPath Press. She was co-editor for *Borderlands: Texas Poetry Review* from 2001-2003, and Poetry Editor and co-publisher of *Cranky Literary Journal* from 2005-2007. Her book reviews and interviews appear in *CutBank Reviews, Gently Read Literature, The International Examiner, Reading Local*, and other publications.

She currently lives in Seattle, where she works at the University of Washington as an accountant.

www.ingramcontent.com/pod-product-compliance
Lightning Source LLC
LaVergne TN
LVHW041517070426
835507LV00012B/1648